Tap the tin

Sid taps the tin.

Tap, tap, tap.

Pam taps the tin.

It is Sid's tin.

Pam and Sid
tap the tin.

Sid taps Pam.
Tap, tap, tap.

The tin is Sid's.

Before reading

Say the sounds: s a t p i n m d

Practise blending the sounds: tap tin Sid Pam Sid's taps

High-frequency words: it and **Tricky words:** the is

Vocabulary check: tap – Have you ever seen a cat or kitten playing with something and tapping it with their paw? What does it look like when something gets tapped? (Demonstrate using your fingers to tap a surface.)

Story discussion: The title and the cover illustration can give us a good idea about the story. Who will be in this story and what do you think might happen?

Teaching points: Teach children about the use of an apostrophe + s to show that a person or thing owns something (the possessive form), e.g. Sid's tin. Use children's names and their belongings as examples. Write some up so that everyone can see.

After reading

Comprehension:
- What was Sid doing with the tin at the start of the story?
- What happened next?
- Why did Sid tap Pam?
- How did the story end?

Fluency: Speed read the words again from the inside front cover.